Jill Calcagno-Russell

DEVELOPING AWARENESS OF SIMILARITIES AND DIFFERENCES

Jean Gilliam DeGaetano
Illustrations by Kevin N. Newman

Great Ideas for Teaching · P.O. Box 444 · Wrightsville Beach · NC · 28480

Copyright 1997 Great Ideas for Teaching, Inc.
All rights reserved. Printed in the U.S.A.
Published by Great Ideas for Teaching, Inc.
P.O. Box 444, Wrightsville Beach, NC 28480

Copies of all materials may be produced for classroom use and homework assignments. Copies may not be produced for entire school districts, used for commercial resale, stored in a retrieval system, or transmitted in any form: electronic, mechanical, recording, etc., without permission from the publisher.

ISBN 1-886143-38-2

DEVELOPING AWARENESS OF SIMILARITIES AND DIFFERENCES

Jean G. DeGaetano and Jeanne A. DeGaetano

Rationale:

Most students have a basic understanding of classification by the time they come to school. They can group clothing, toys, food, furniture, etc. They also have a basic understanding of classifying by uses, such as things a teacher uses, things that are used for cooking, things that are used for writing, etc.

While the majority of students grasp classification of more subtle similarities and/or differences by hearing, observing and communicating, other students frequently need direct one-to-one repetitious practice to develop a full understanding of subtle similarities that place various objects, people or animals in the same grouping. They need to learn that one object, animal or person can be part of numerous groupings or classifications. With repetitious practice, using the same pictures, they soon understand why certain things can be grouped by a similar characteristic, such as, grouped with other animals when the grouping is "animals," grouped with many of the same animals when the grouping is "animals that live on a farm," grouped with others, such as "animals that live on a farm and provide people with food or drink," then quickly separated when the category might change to "animals that live in the farmer's house" or "animals that are smaller than a collie dog."

Directions for Use:

The pages in the book are intended to serve as reproducible masters. Make as many copies of each page as needed. Copies may be made ahead and stored for convenient use. Each student's worksheet has an instructor's worksheet. Each statement on the instructor's worksheet is to be read aloud to the students, allowing adequate time for the students to mark their papers. Statements should be repeated, if necessary, or additional explanations given.

Variation: Make extra copies of the pages and cut the pictures apart. Encourage the students to make new categories by observing similar characteristics or uses.

This note may be copied and attached to both the student's copy and the instructor's copy when sending work home:

Student's Name: _____

We are learning about similarities and differences that group objects, animals and people together. The student's paper and the instructor's paper are attached, showing what was read aloud to the student and how the student responded to the statement. Thank you for reviewing your child's work.

_____

Name: _____   **Date:** _____

  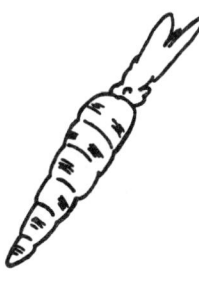 

Great Ideas for Teaching, Inc.   1   Developing Awareness of Similarities and Differences

Instructor's Worksheet

1. A cat has fur. Circle another thing that has fur.

2. A cow lives on a farm. Circle another thing that lives on a farm.

  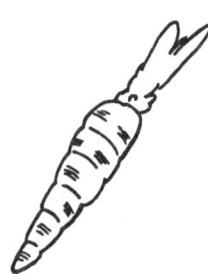 

3. A banana is yellow. Circle another thing that is yellow.

4. Leaves grow on a tree. Circle another thing that grows on a tree.

Great Ideas for Teaching, Inc.

Developing Awareness of Similarities and Differences

Name: _____ Date: _____

Great Ideas for Teaching, Inc.   3   Developing Awareness of Similarities and Differences

Instructor's Worksheet

1. A fire engine has a siren. Circle another thing that has a siren.

  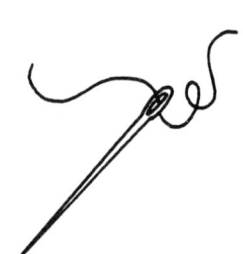 

2. A nail is sharp. Circle another thing that is sharp.

3. A table has four legs. Circle another thing that has four legs.

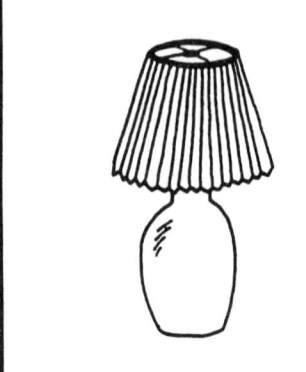   

4. A lamp gives off light. Circle another thing that gives off light.

Great Ideas for Teaching, Inc.

Developing Awareness of Similarities and Differences

Name: _____ Date: _____

Great Ideas for Teaching, Inc.

Developing Awareness of Similarities and Differences

Instructor's Worksheet

1. A car has tires. Circle another thing that has tires.

2. Fish live in water. Circle another thing that lives in water.

3. A wagon has four wheels. Circle another thing that has four wheels.

4. A ghost is scary. Circle another thing that is scary.

Great Ideas for Teaching, Inc.

Developing Awareness of Similarities and Differences

Name: _____ Date: _____

Great Ideas for Teaching, Inc.

7

Developing Awareness of Similarities and Differences

Instructor's Worksheet

1. An elf is make-believe. Circle another thing that is make-believe.

2. Ice skates have laces. Circle another thing that has laces.

3. A mouse has a long tail. Circle another thing that has a long tail.

4. A harp has strings. Circle another thing that has strings.

Great Ideas for Teaching, Inc.　　　　Developing Awareness of Similarities and Differences

Name: _____ Date: _____

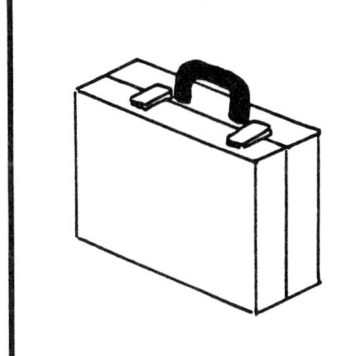 

Great Ideas for Teaching, Inc.   9   Developing Awareness of Similarities and Differences

Instructor's Worksheet

  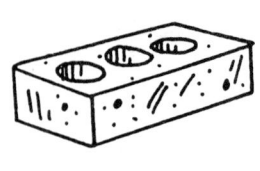 

1. A rock is hard. Circle another thing that is hard.

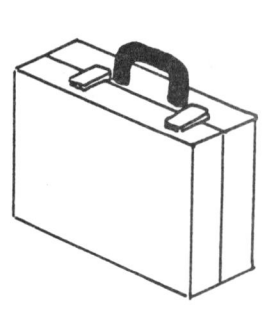   

2. A suitcase opens and closes. Circle another thing that opens and closes.

3. A rabbit has whiskers. Circle another thing that has whiskers.

 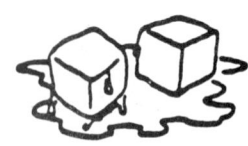  

4. An iron is hot. Circle another thing that is hot.

Great Ideas for Teaching, Inc.

Developing Awareness of Similarities and Differences

Name: _____   Date: _____

Great Ideas for Teaching, Inc.

Developing Awareness of Similarities and Differences

Instructor's Worksheet

1. A rake has prongs. Circle another thing that has prongs.

2. A cage has bars. Circle another thing that has bars.

3. A bear has claws. Circle another thing that has claws.

4. A frog can hop. Circle another thing that can hop.

Name: _____ **Date:** _____

   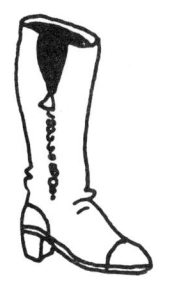

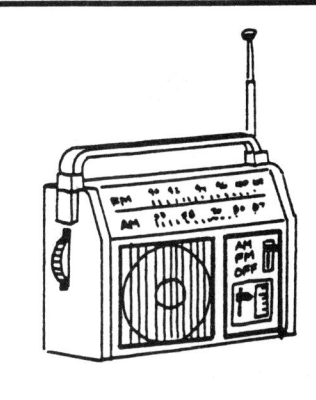   

Great Ideas for Teaching, Inc.

Developing Awareness of Similarities and Differences

Instructor's Worksheet

1. Ice cream is cold. Circle another thing that is cold.

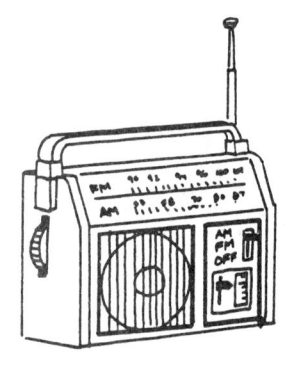   

2. A radio can play music. Circle another thing that plays music.

3. Cookies are baked in an oven. Circle another thing that is baked in an oven.

   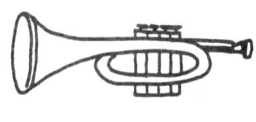

4. A drum is a musical instrument. Circle another thing that is a musical instrument.

Great Ideas for Teaching, Inc.

Developing Awareness of Similarities and Differences

Name: _____   Date: _____

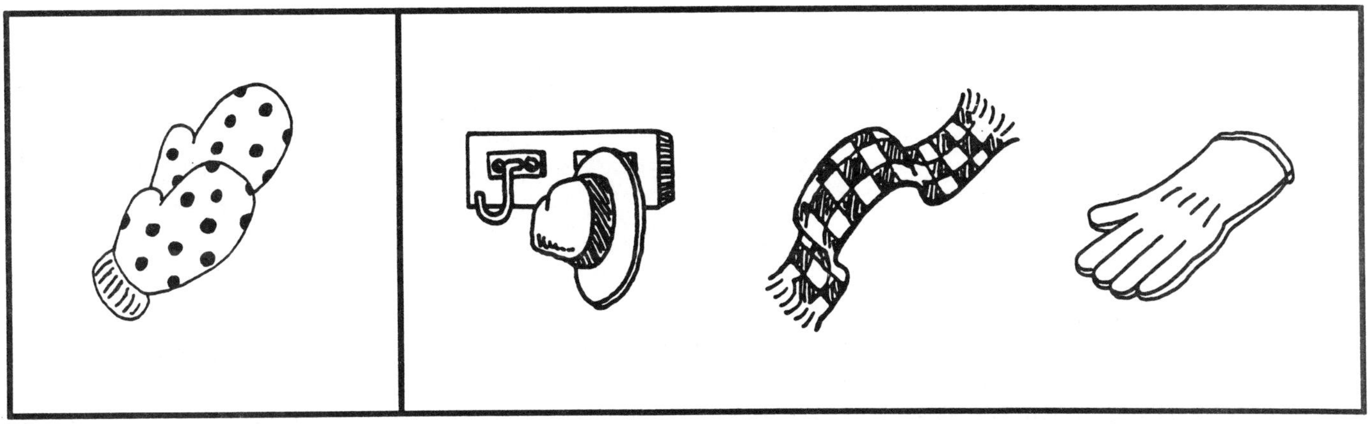

Great Ideas for Teaching, Inc.   15   Developing Awareness of Similarities and Differences

Instructor's Worksheet

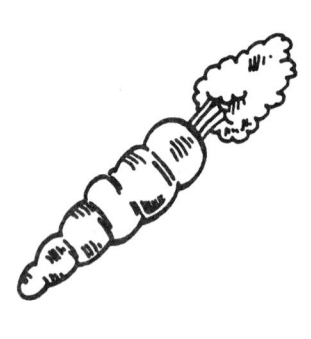   

1. A carrot is orange. Circle another thing that is orange.

2. A rope can pull things. Circle another object that can pull things.

3. A mailman wears a uniform. Circle another person that wears a uniform.

4. Mittens can keep your hands warm. Circle another thing that can keep your hands warm.

Name: _____ Date: _____

Great Ideas for Teaching, Inc.   17   Developing Awareness of Similarities and Differences

Instructor's Worksheet

1. Honey is sticky. Circle another thing that is sticky.

 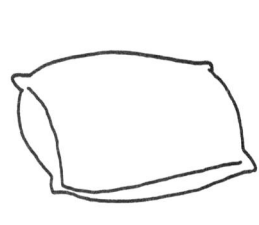  

2. A robot is made of metal. Circle another thing made of metal.

3. A sheep is soft and fluffy. Circle another thing that is soft and fluffy.

4. You can see a clown at the circus. Circle another thing you might see at a circus.

Great Ideas for Teaching, Inc. Developing Awareness of Similarities and Differences

Name: _____ Date: _____

 |

 |

 |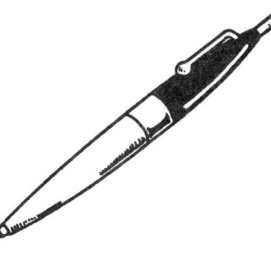

 |

Great Ideas for Teaching, Inc.   19   <u>Developing Awareness of Similarities and Differences</u>

Instructor's Worksheet

1. A goat has horns. Circle another thing that has horns.

2. A bird has feathers. Circle another thing that has feathers.

   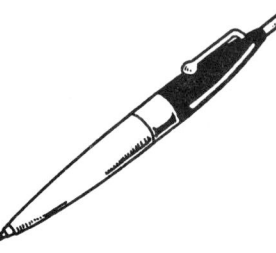

3. You can write with a pencil. Circle another thing that you can write with.

4. A trunk is part of a tree. Circle another thing that is part of a tree.

Great Ideas for Teaching, Inc.

Developing Awareness of Similarities and Differences

Name: _____   Date: _____

Great Ideas for Teaching, Inc.   Developing Awareness of Similarities and Differences

Instructor's Worksheet

1. A tiger has stripes. Circle another thing that has stripes.

2. An alligator has short legs. Circle another thing that has short legs.

3. A cupcake has frosting. Circle another thing that has frosting.

4. A bus has many wheels. Circle another thing that has many wheels.

Great Ideas for Teaching, Inc.

Developing Awareness of Similarities and Differences

Name: _____ Date: _____

Great Ideas for Teaching, Inc.   23   Developing Awareness of Similarities and Differences

Instructor's Worksheet

1. A duck has webbed feet. Circle another thing that has webbed feet.

2. Apples can be used to make a pie. Circle another thing that can be used to make a pie.

3. You can see the moon in the sky at night. Circle another thing you can see in the sky at night.

4. A nail can be used to hang things on a wall. Circle another thing that can be used to hang something on a wall.

Great Ideas for Teaching, Inc.   Developing Awareness of Similarities and Differences

Name: _____ Date: _____

Great Ideas for Teaching, Inc.   25   Developing Awareness of Similarities and Differences

Instructor's Worksheet

1. A monkey has a curly tail. Circle another thing that has a curly tail.

2. A lifeguard uses a whistle. Circle another person that uses a whistle.

3. An orange is very juicy. Circle another thing that is very juicy.

4. Books can be found in a classroom. Circle another thing that can be found in a classroom.

Great Ideas for Teaching, Inc.

Developing Awareness of Similarities and Differences

Name: _____ Date: _____

 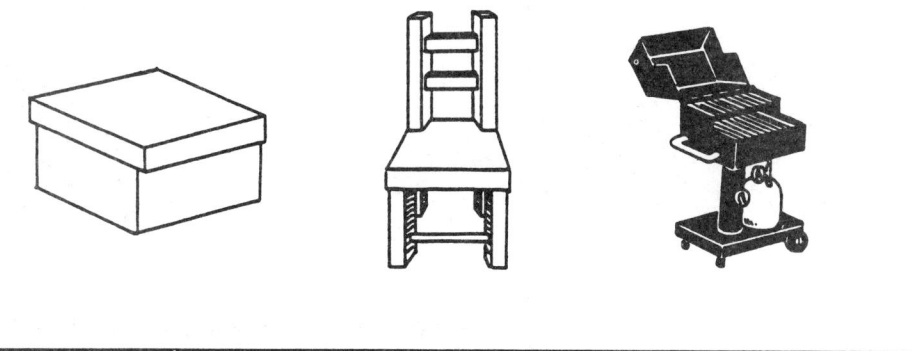

 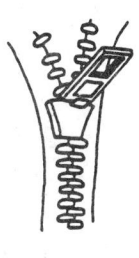  

Great Ideas for Teaching, Inc. 27 Developing Awareness of Similarities and Differences

Instructor's Worksheet

1. A panda bear is black and white. Circle another thing that is black and white.

2. A watermelon has seeds in it. Circle another thing that has seeds in it.

 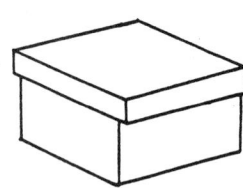 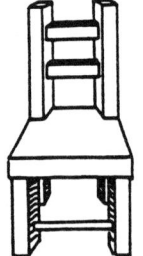 

3. Food can be cooked on a stove. Circle another thing that food can be cooked on.

 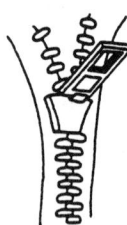  

4. Buttons can keep a coat closed. Circle another thing that can keep a coat closed.

Great Ideas for Teaching, Inc.

Developing Awareness of Similarities and Differences

Name: _____ Date: _____

Great Ideas for Teaching, Inc. 29 Developing Awareness of Similarities and Differences

Instructor's Worksheet

1. A snail carries a shell on its back. Circle another thing that carries a shell on its back.

2. A lollipop has a stick. Circle another thing that has a stick.

3. A tie can be worn around your neck. Circle another thing that can be worn around your neck.

   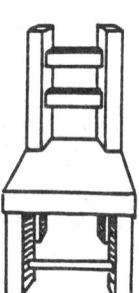

4. A clock tells the time. Circle another thing that tells the time.

Great Ideas for Teaching, Inc.

Developing Awareness of Similarities and Differences

Name: _____ Date: _____

  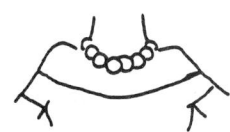 

Great Ideas for Teaching, Inc.   31   Developing Awareness of Similarities and Differences

Instructor's Worksheet

1. A dog can be a good pet. Circle another thing that can be a good pet.

2. A pumpkin grows on a vine. Circle another thing that grows on a vine.

3. Cowboys wear boots. Circle another thing that cowboys wear.

4. A radio has an antenna. Circle another thing that has an antenna.

Great Ideas for Teaching, Inc.

Developing Awareness of Similarities and Differences

Name: _____ Date: _____

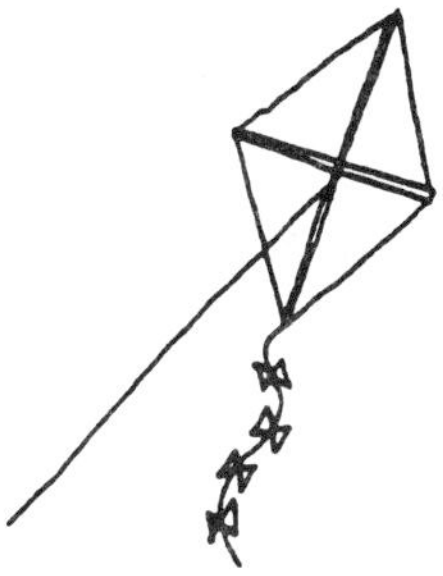

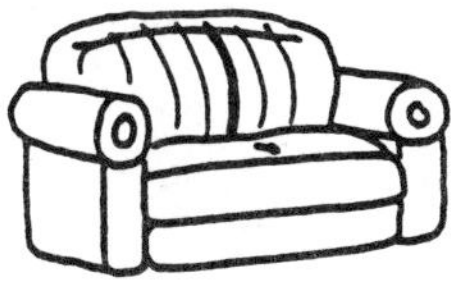

Great Ideas for Teaching, Inc.   33   Developing Awareness of Similarities and Differences

Instructor's Worksheet

1. A crab has sharp claws. Circle another thing that has sharp claws.

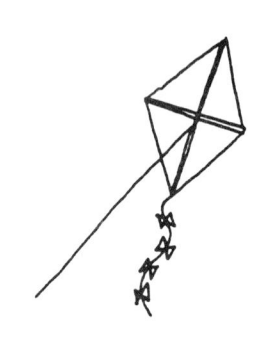   

2. A kite flies high in the sky. Circle another thing that flies high in the sky.

 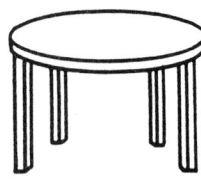  

3. A rocking chair rocks back and forth. Circle another thing that rocks back and forth.

4. A walrus has tusks. Circle another thing that has tusks.

Great Ideas for Teaching, Inc.

Developing Awareness of Similarities and Differences

Name: _____ Date: _____

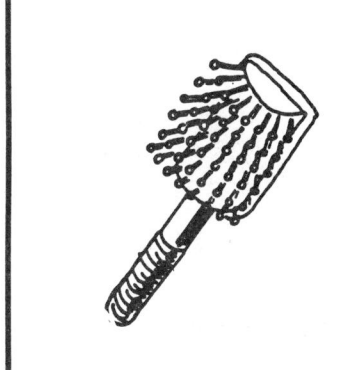  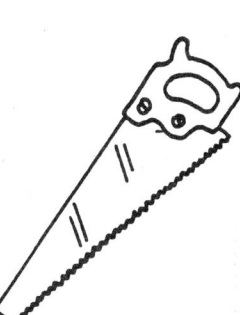 

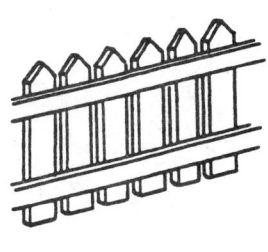   

Great Ideas for Teaching, Inc.   35   Developing Awareness of Similarities and Differences

Instructor's Worksheet

1. A hairdresser uses a brush to style your hair. Circle another thing that can be used to style your hair.

2. An elephant has big ears. Circle another thing that has big ears.

3. A sliding board is slippery. Circle another thing that is slippery.

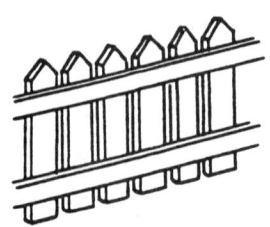   

4. A fence can be made of wood. Circle another thing that can be made of wood.

Great Ideas for Teaching, Inc. Developing Awareness of Similarities and Differences

Name: _____ Date: _____

Great Ideas for Teaching, Inc.   37   Developing Awareness of Similarities and Differences

Instructor's Worksheet

1. A saw can be used to cut wood. Circle another thing that can be used to cut wood.

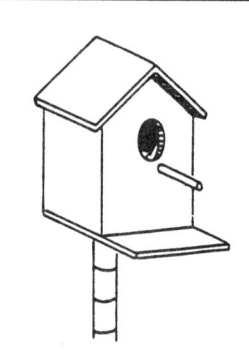 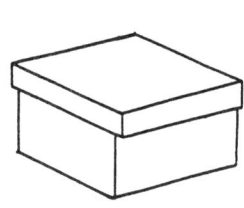  

2. A bird can live in a birdhouse. Circle another thing that a bird can live in.

  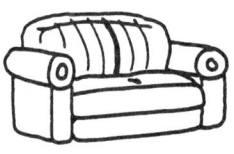 

3. A windmill can blow air. Circle another thing that blows air.

4. An apple has a stem. Circle another thing that has a stem.

Great Ideas for Teaching, Inc. 38 Developing Awareness of Similarities and Differences

Name: _____ Date: _____

Great Ideas for Teaching, Inc.   39   Developing Awareness of Similarities and Differences

Instructor's Worksheet

1. A queen wears a crown. Circle another person who wears a crown.

2. A seal likes to play in the water. Circle another thing that likes to play in the water.

3. A vacuum cleaner can be used to clean a floor. Circle another thing that can be used to clean a floor.

4. A snake crawls along the ground. Circle another thing that crawls along the ground.

Great Ideas for Teaching, Inc. 40 Developing Awareness of Similarities and Differences

Name: _____ **Date:** _____

  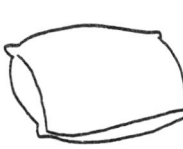 

Great Ideas for Teaching, Inc.   41   Developing Awareness of Similarities and Differences

Instructor's Worksheet

1. A bee can fly. Circle two other things that can fly.

2. A turtle moves slowly. Circle two other things that move slowly.

  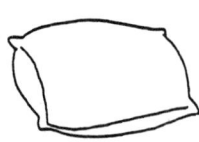 

3. A kitten is very soft. Circle two other things that are soft.

4. An octopus has many legs. Circle two other things that have many legs.

Great Ideas for Teaching, Inc.

Developing Awareness of Similarities and Differences

Name: _____ Date: _____

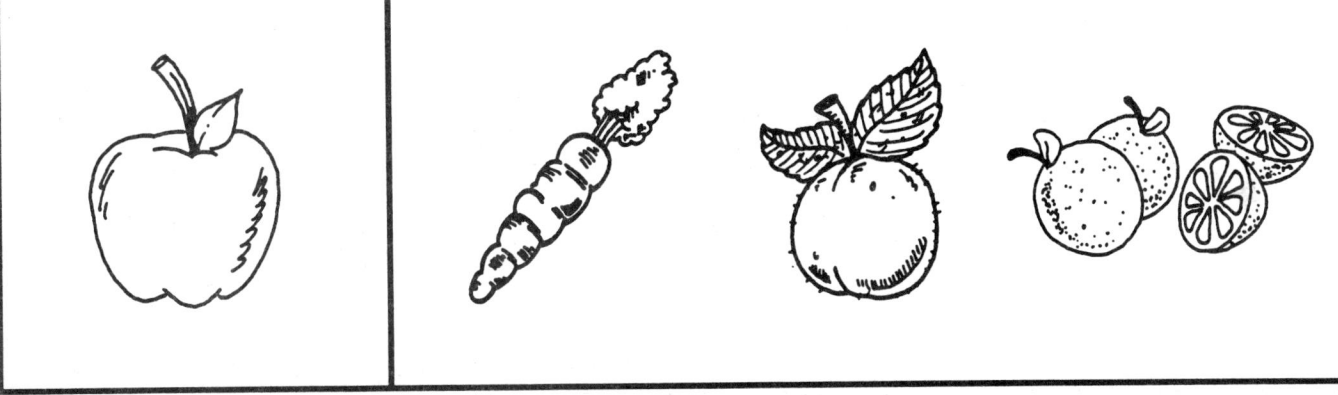

Great Ideas for Teaching, Inc.　　　43　　　Developing Awareness of Similarities and Differences

Instructor's Worksheet

1. Soup is served hot. Circle two other things that are served hot.

2. Apples grow on trees. Circle two other things that grow on trees.

3. Ketchup comes in a bottle. Circle two other things that come in bottles.

4. Carrots grow in a garden. Circle two other things that grow in a garden.

Great Ideas for Teaching, Inc.

Developing Awareness of Similarities and Differences

Name: _____ Date: _____

Great Ideas for Teaching, Inc.   45   Developing Awareness of Similarities and Differences

Instructor's Worksheet

1. A train can be used to haul things. Circle two other things that can be used to haul objects.

 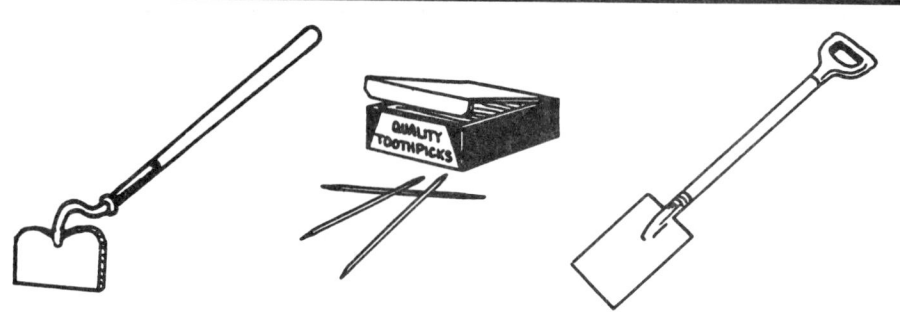

2. A rake is a tool you can use in a garden. Circle two other things that can be used in a garden.

   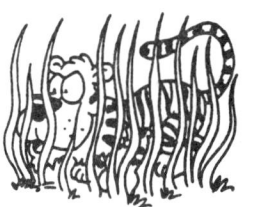

3. A shark has sharp teeth. Circle two other things that have sharp teeth.

 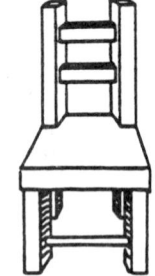 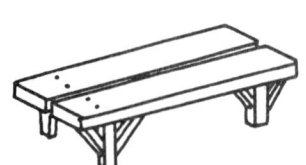 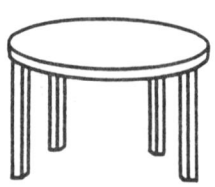

4. People can sit on a sofa. Circle two other things that people can sit on.

Great Ideas for Teaching, Inc. Developing Awareness of Similarities and Differences

Name: _____ Date: _____

Great Ideas for Teaching, Inc.

Developing Awareness of Similarities and Differences

Instructor's Worksheet

1. Soup can be eaten with a spoon. Circle two other things that can be eaten with a spoon.

2. A frog can jump high. Circle two other things that can jump high.

3. A strawberry is a piece of fruit. Circle two other pieces of fruit.

4. A house has windows. Circle two other things that are part of a house.

Great Ideas for Teaching, Inc.

Developing Awareness of Similarities and Differences

Name: _____ Date: _____

Great Ideas for Teaching, Inc.　　　49　　　Developing Awareness of Similarities and Differences

Instructor's Worksheet

1. A guitar is a musical instrument. Circle two other things that are musical instruments.

2. A table has four legs. Circle two other things that have four legs.

3. A drawer opens and closes. Circle two other things that open and close.

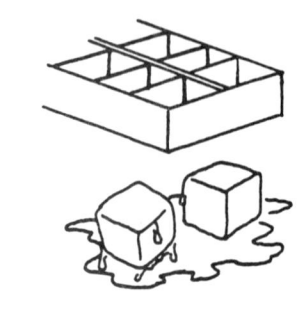   

4. An ice cube can melt in the sun. Circle two other things that can melt in the sun.

Developing Awareness of Similarities and Differences

Name: _____ Date: _____

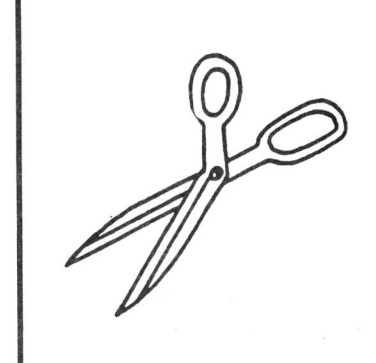 

Great Ideas for Teaching, Inc.   51   Developing Awareness of Similarities and Differences

Instructor's Worksheet

1. A lion can live in a zoo. Circle two other things that can live in a zoo.

2. Scissors are very sharp. Circle two other things that are very sharp.

3. A dress is a piece of clothing. Circle two other things that are pieces of clothing.

4. A pirate is scary. Circle two other things that are scary.

Great Ideas for Teaching, Inc. Developing Awareness of Similarities and Differences

Name: _____ Date: _____

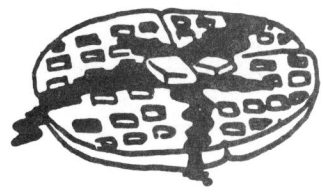

Great Ideas for Teaching, Inc.   53   Developing Awareness of Similarities and Differences

Instructor's Worksheet

1. A giant is very big. Circle two other things that are very big.

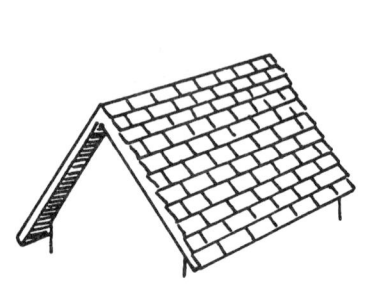   

2. A roof is part of a house. Circle two other things that are part of a house.

3. An angel has wings. Circle two other things that have wings.

4. You can eat toast for breakfast. Circle two other things that you can eat for breakfast.

Name: _____ Date: _____

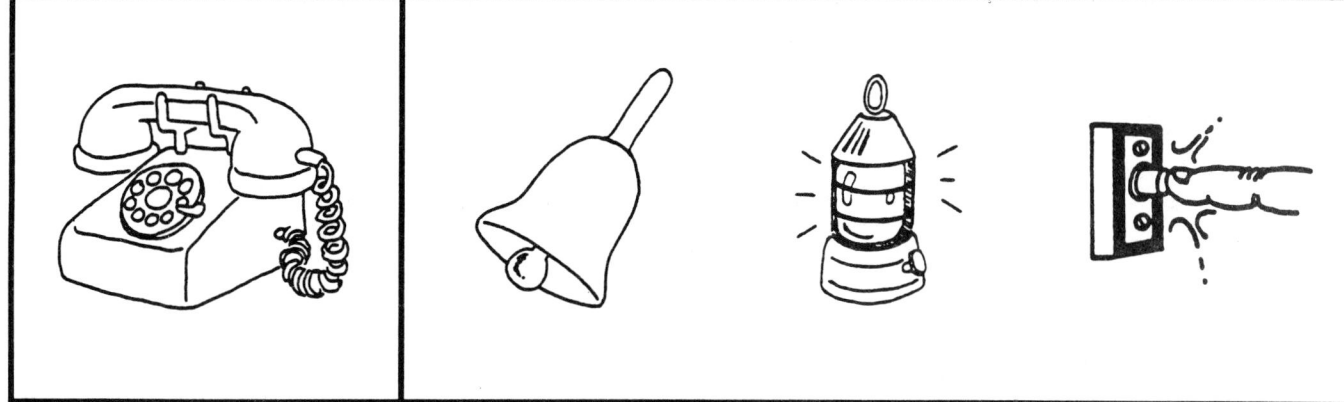

  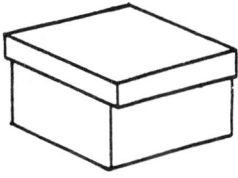 

Great Ideas for Teaching, Inc.   55   <u>Developing Awareness of Similarities and Differences</u>

Instructor's Worksheet

 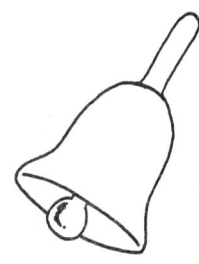  

1. A telephone makes a ringing sound. Circle two other things that make ringing sounds.

2. A seashell can be found at the beach. Circle two other things that can be found at the beach.

  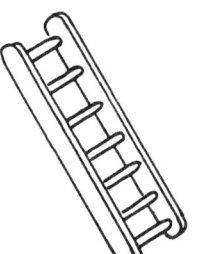 

3. A seesaw goes up and down. Circle two other things that go up and down.

  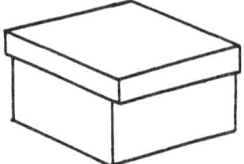 

4. A pot has a lid. Circle two other things that have a lid.

Name: _____ Date: _____

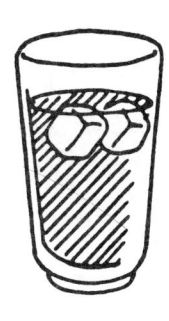

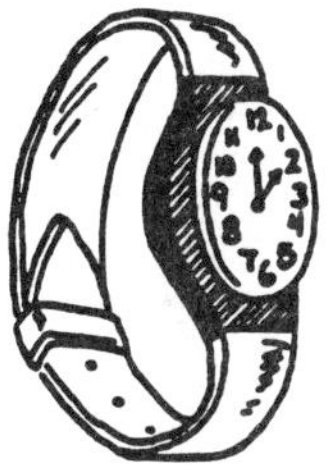

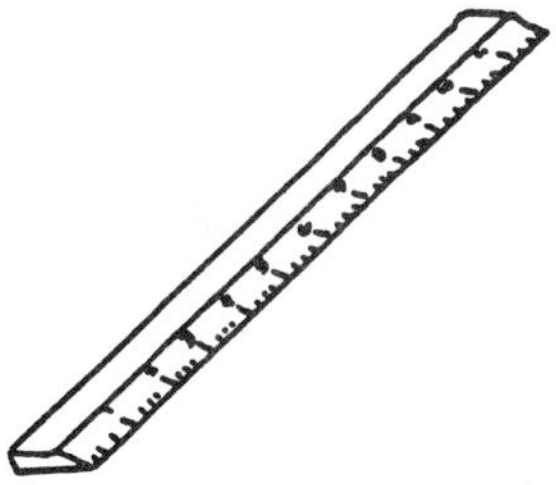

Great Ideas for Teaching, Inc. 57 Developing Awareness of Similarities and Differences

Instructor's Worksheet

1. Ice cream is a good dessert. Circle two other things that are good desserts.

2. A telephone has numbers on it. Circle two other things that have numbers on them.

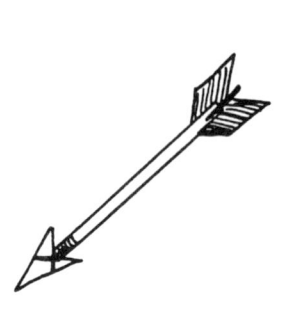  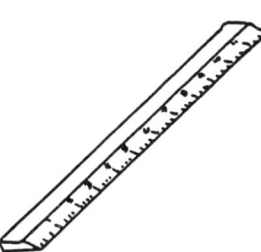 

3. An arrow is straight. Circle two other things that are straight.

4. A glass is breakable. Circle two other things that are breakable.

Great Ideas for Teaching, Inc.   Developing Awareness of Similarities and Differences

Name: _____ Date: _____

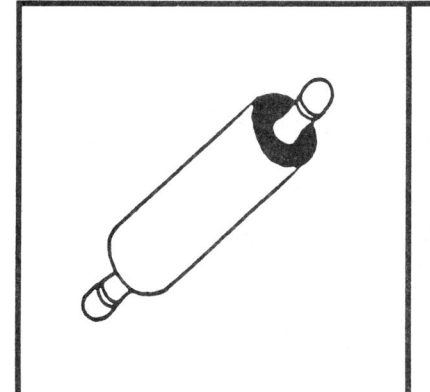 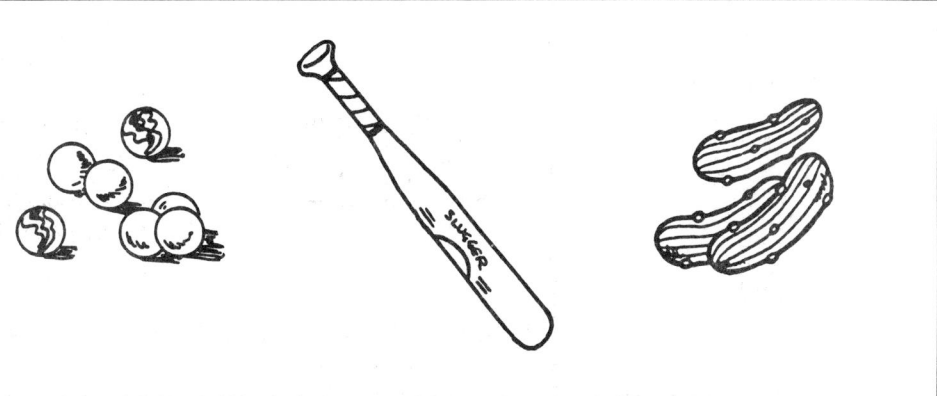

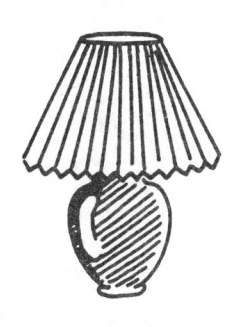  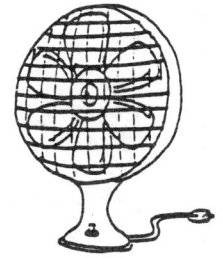 

Instructor's Worksheet

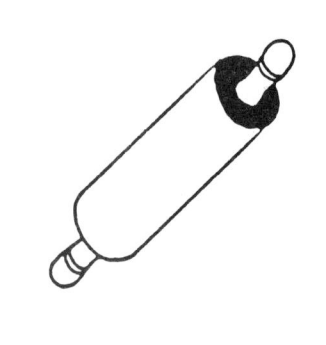
  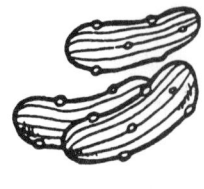

1. A rolling pin is **smooth**. Circle two other things that are smooth.

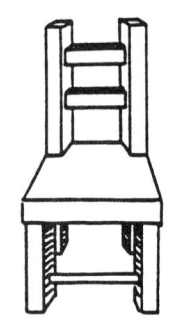  

2. A jack-in-the-box is a **toy**. Circle two other things that are toys.

3. An apple has a **stem**. Circle two other things that have a stem.

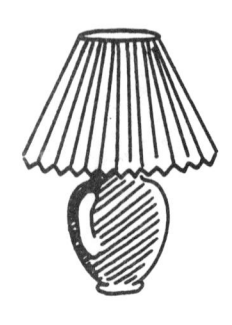
 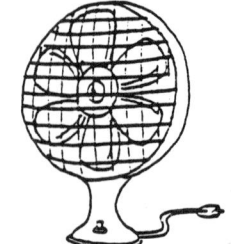 

4. A lamp can be **switched on and off**. Circle two other things that can be switched on and off.

Great Ideas for Teaching, Inc.

Developing Awareness of Similarities and Differences

Name: _____ Date: _____

Great Ideas for Teaching, Inc. 61 Developing Awareness of Similarities and Differences

Instructor's Worksheet

1. An elephant is very big. Circle two other things that are very big.

2. People can drink from a glass. Circle two other things people can drink from.

   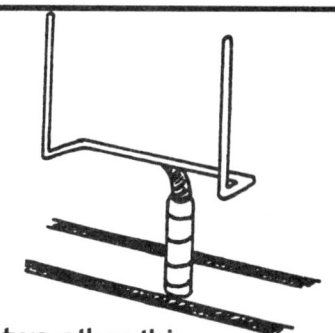

3. A football player needs a helmet. Circle two other things a football player needs.

 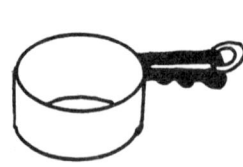  

4. A basket can have a handle. Circle two other things that have a handle.

Great Ideas for Teaching, Inc.

Developing Awareness of Similarities and Differences

Name: _____   Date: _____

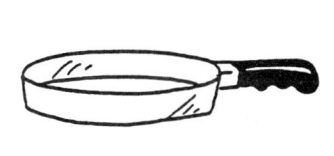 

 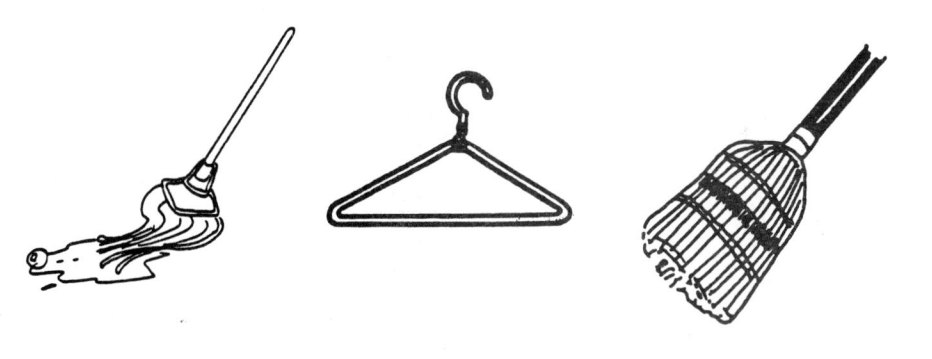

Great Ideas for Teaching, Inc.

Developing Awareness of Similarities and Differences

Instructor's Worksheet

1. A cat has whiskers. Circle two other things that have whiskers.

  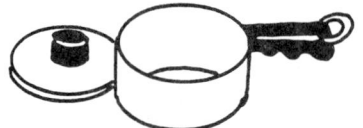 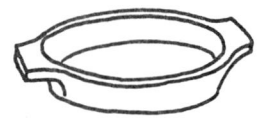

2. You can use a frying pan to cook food. Circle two other things that can be used to cook food.

 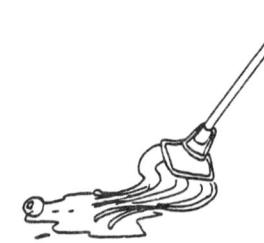  

3. You can use a dustpan when you clean a house. Circle two other things you can use when you clean a house.

4. A dog has a tail. Circle two other things that have a tail.

Great Ideas for Teaching, Inc.

Developing Awareness of Similarities and Differences

Name: _____ Date: _____

 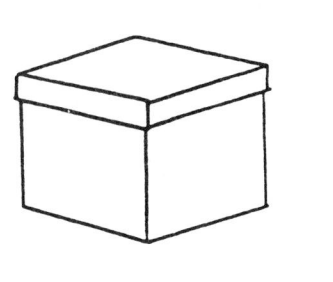  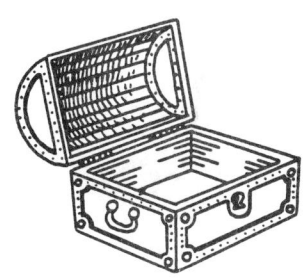

Great Ideas for Teaching, Inc.   65   Developing Awareness of Similarities and Differences

Instructor's Worksheet

1. A camel can carry things on its back. Circle two other animals that can carry things on their backs.

2. A basketball player uses a ball when he plays. Circle two other people who use a ball when they play.

 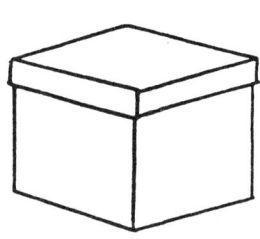  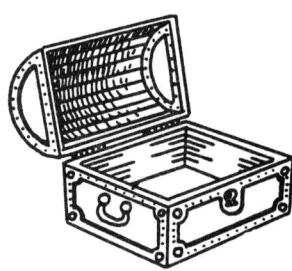

3. A basket can hold things. Circle two other objects that can hold things.

4. Grass is green. Circle two other things that are green.

Great Ideas for Teaching, Inc.   Developing Awareness of Similarities and Differences

Name: _____ Date: _____

Great Ideas for Teaching, Inc.　　67　　Developing Awareness of Similarities and Differences

Instructor's Worksheet

1. A ship can sail on the water. Circle two other things that can sail on the water.

2. Smoke comes from a fire. Circle two other things smoke can come from.

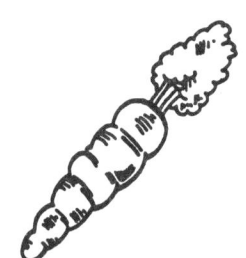

3. An apple is red. Circle two other things that are red.

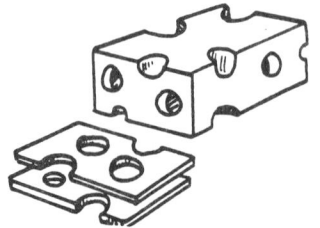

4. A net has holes in it. Circle two other things that have holes in them.

Great Ideas for Teaching, Inc. Developing Awareness of Similarities and Differences

Name: _____ Date: _____

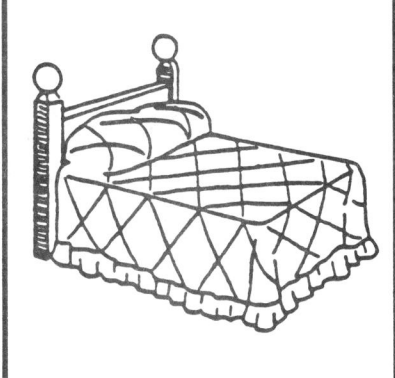 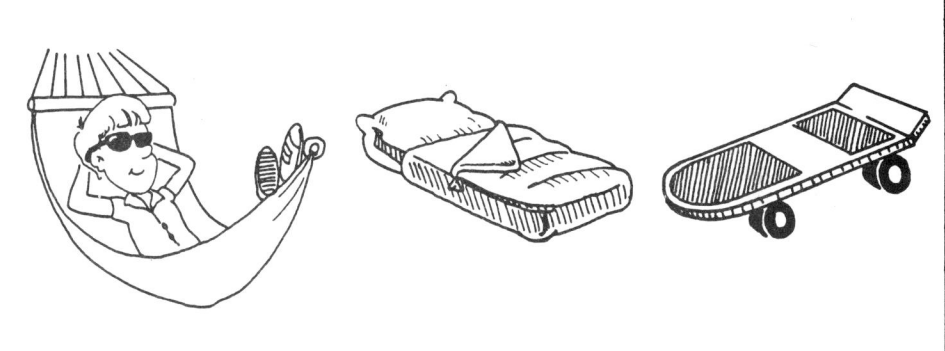

Great Ideas for Teaching, Inc. 69 Developing Awareness of Similarities and Differences

Instructor's Worksheet

1. A cow lives in a barn. Circle two other things that live in a barn.

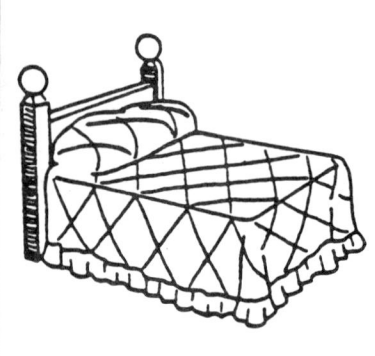 

2. A person can sleep in a bed. Circle two other places where people can sleep.

 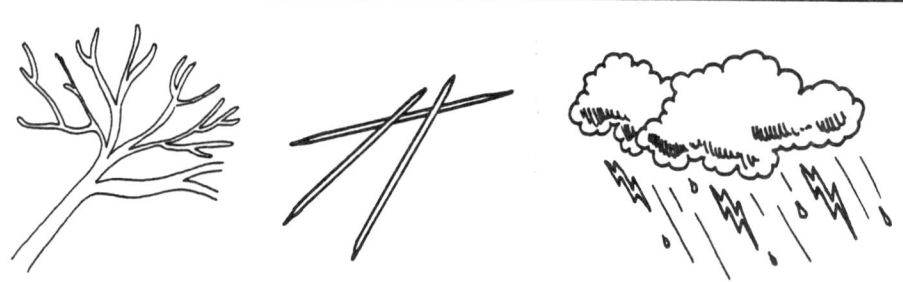

3. A road can be crooked. Circle two other things that can be crooked.

4. A car needs gasoline to make it run. Circle two other things that need gasoline to make them run.

Great Ideas for Teaching, Inc.   Developing Awareness of Similarities and Differences

Name: _____ Date: _____

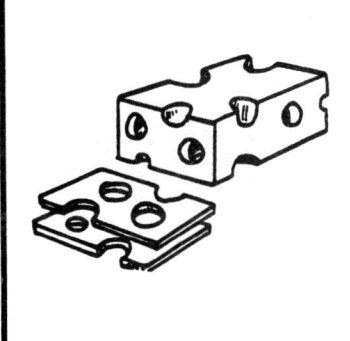   

Great Ideas for Teaching, Inc.

Developing Awareness of Similarities and Differences

Instructor's Worksheet

1. An elephant is heavy. Circle two other things that are heavy.

2. A scarecrow is stuffed. Circle two other things that are stuffed.

3. An elf is tiny. Circle two other things that are tiny.

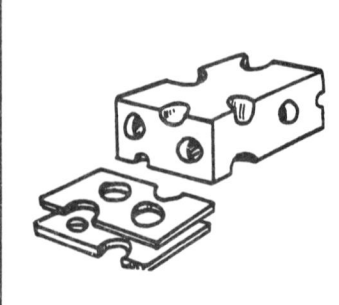   

4. Cheese can be sliced. Circle two other things that can be sliced.

Great Ideas for Teaching, Inc.　　　Developing Awareness of Similarities and Differences

Name: _____ Date: _____

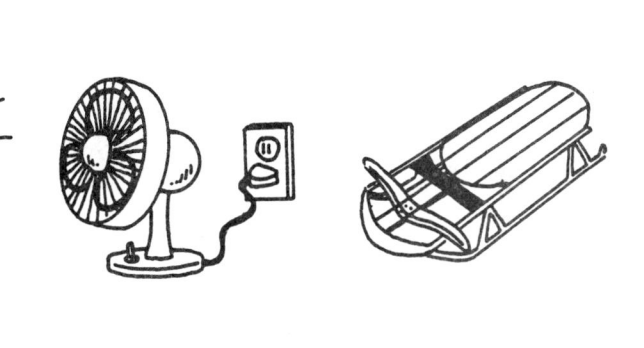

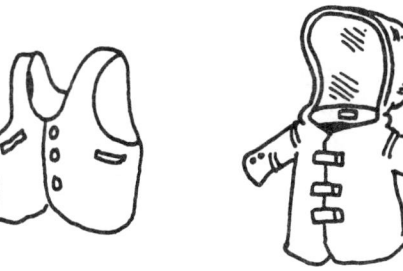

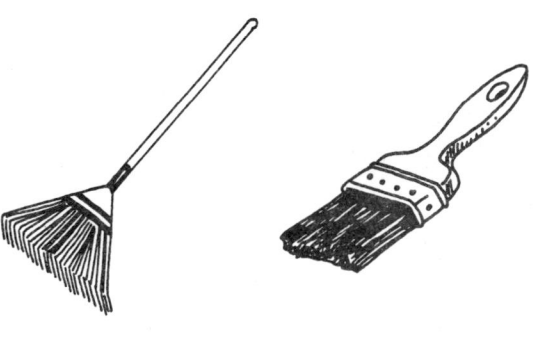

Great Ideas for Teaching, Inc.   73   Developing Awareness of Similarities and Differences

Instructor's Worksheet

1. A tractor moves slowly. Circle two other things that move slowly.

   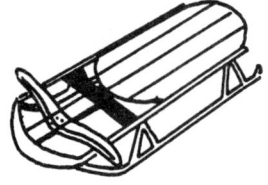

2. Ice skates have blades. Circle two other things that have blades.

3. A shirt can have long sleeves. Circle two other things that have long sleeves.

4. An umbrella has a long handle. Circle two other things that have a long handle.

Name: _____ Date: _____

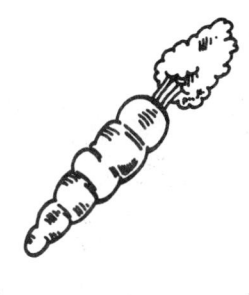

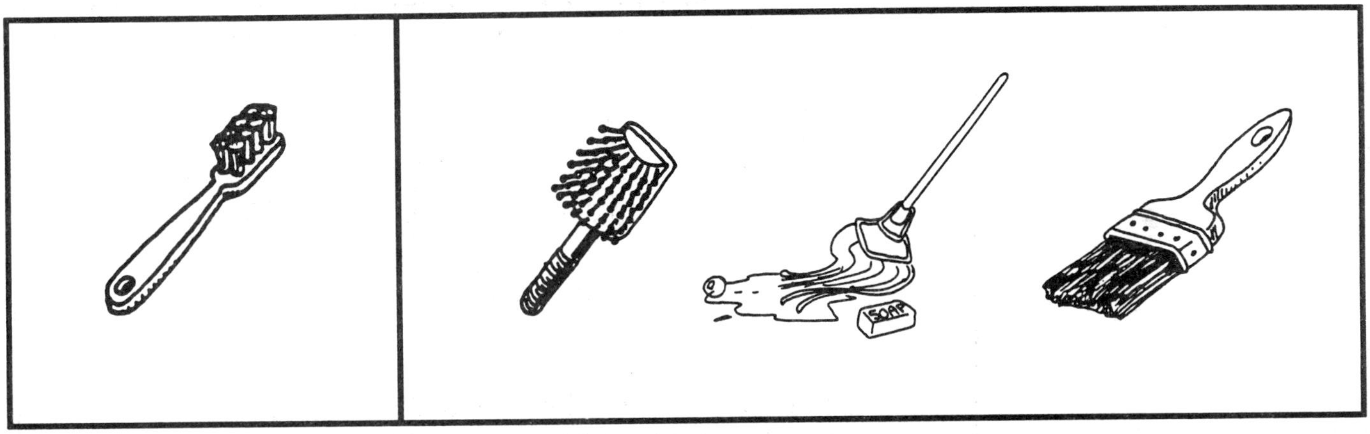

Great Ideas for Teaching, Inc.

75

Developing Awareness of Similarities and Differences

Instructor's Worksheet

   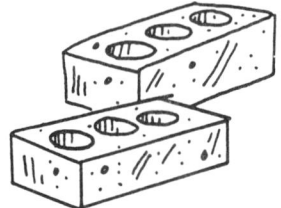

1. A ball is round. Circle two other things that are round.

2. A toothbrush has bristles. Circle two other things that have bristles.

3. An iceberg floats in the water. Circle two other things that float in the water.

4. A pumpkin is orange. Circle two other things that are orange.

Great Ideas for Teaching, Inc.

Developing Awareness of Similarities and Differences

Name: _____ Date: _____

Great Ideas for Teaching, Inc.   77   Developing Awareness of Similarities and Differences

Instructor's Worksheet

   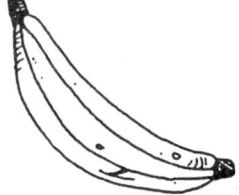

1. An apple is crunchy. Circle two other things that are crunchy.

2. A squirrel can climb a tree. Circle two other things that can climb a tree.

3. A torch has a flame. Circle two other things that have a flame.

4. You can see a star in the sky. Circle two other things that you can see in the sky.

Great Ideas for Teaching, Inc. Developing Awareness of Similarities and Differences

Name: _____ Date: _____

Great Ideas for Teaching, Inc.   79   Developing Awareness of Similarities and Differences

Instructor's Worksheet

1. Bread is made of flour. Circle two other things that are made of flour.

2. You can buy cookies in a bakery. Circle two other things that you can buy in a bakery.

3. An octopus has many legs. Circle two other things that have many legs.

   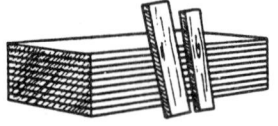

4. You can build things with blocks. Circle two other objects that you can use to build things.

Great Ideas for Teaching, Inc. Developing Awareness of Similarities and Differences

Name: _____ Date: _____

   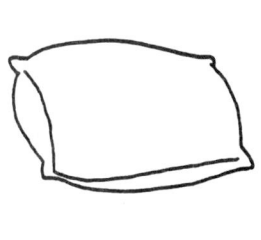

Great Ideas for Teaching, Inc.

Developing Awareness of Similarities and Differences

Instructor's Worksheet

1. A kitten is soft. Circle something that is not soft.

2. A giraffe has a long neck. Circle something that does not have a long neck.

3. A polar bear lives in a very cold place. Circle something that does not live in a cold place.

4. A hamburger can be eaten with your hands. Circle something that cannot be eaten with your hands.

Name: _____ Date: _____

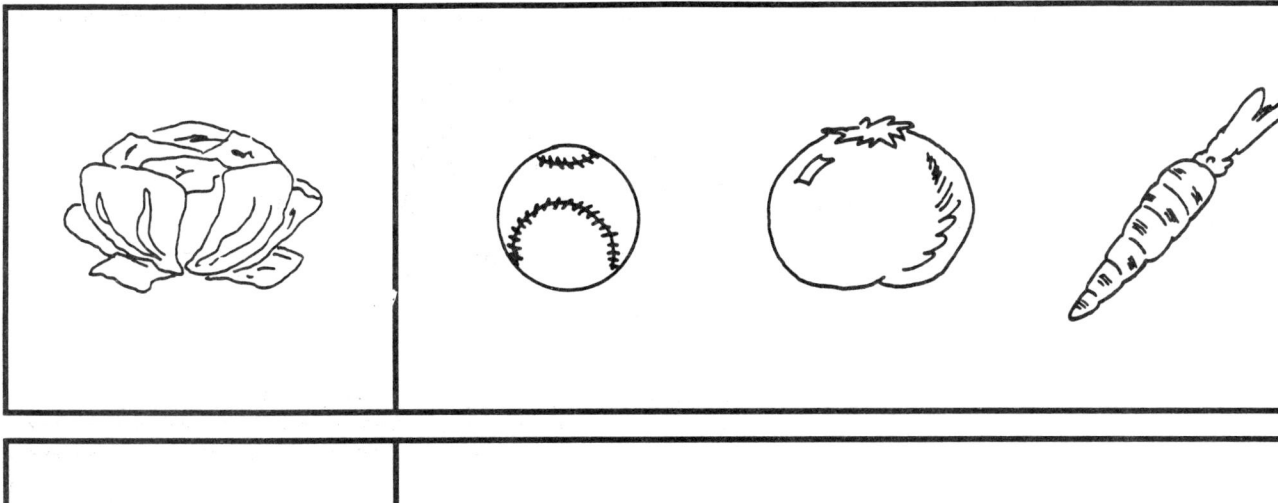

Great Ideas for Teaching, Inc.   83   <u>Developing Awareness of Similarities and Differences</u>

Instructor's Worksheet

 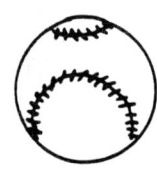  

1. Lettuce is used to make a salad. Circle something that is not used to make a salad.

2. Marshmallows can be roasted over a fire. Circle something that cannot be roasted over a fire.

3. A bird can fly. Circle something that cannot fly.

4. A fire is hot. Circle something that is not hot.

Great Ideas for Teaching, Inc. Developing Awareness of Similarities and Differences

Name: _____ Date: _____

Great Ideas for Teaching, Inc.   85   Developing Awareness of Similarities and Differences

Instructor's Worksheet

1. A car travels on a highway. Circle something that does not travel on a highway.

2. A nurse works in a hospital. Circle someone who does not work in a hospital.

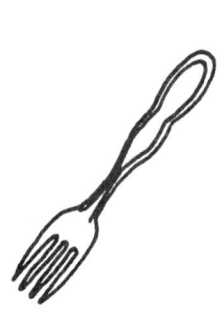 

3. People can use a fork to eat food. Circle something people cannot use to eat with.

4. A fireman uses a ladder. Circle someone who does not use a ladder.

Great Ideas for Teaching, Inc.

Developing Awareness of Similarities and Differences

Name: _____   Date: _____

Great Ideas for Teaching, Inc.   87   Developing Awareness of Similarities and Differences

Instructor's Worksheet

1. A monkey likes to sit in a tree. Circle something that does not like to sit in a tree.

2. A snowman is made out of snow. Circle something that is not made out of snow.

3. A man can wear pants. Circle something that cannot wear pants.

 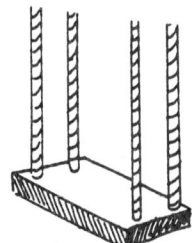 

4. A seesaw can be found on a playground. Circle something that is not found on a playground.

Great Ideas for Teaching, Inc.

Developing Awareness of Similarities and Differences

Name: _____ Date: _____

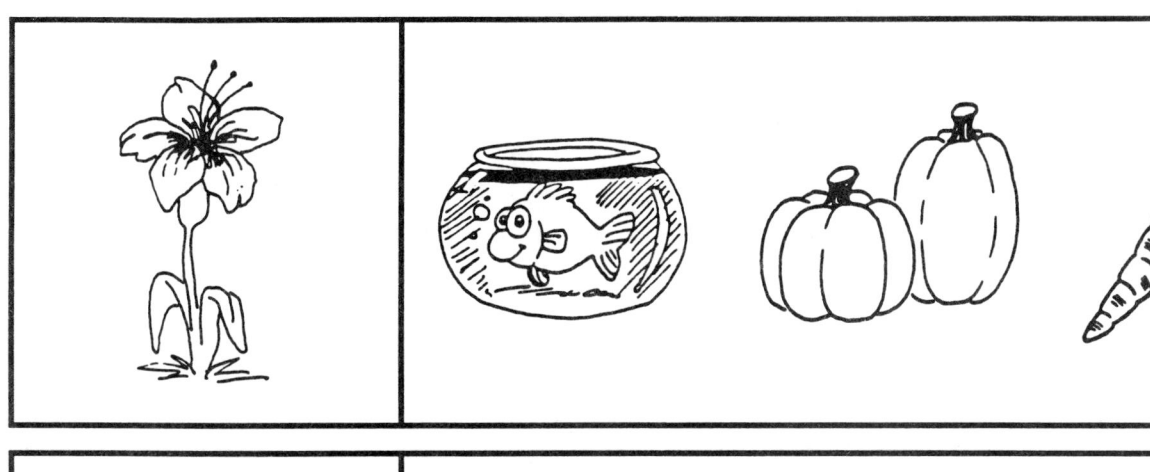

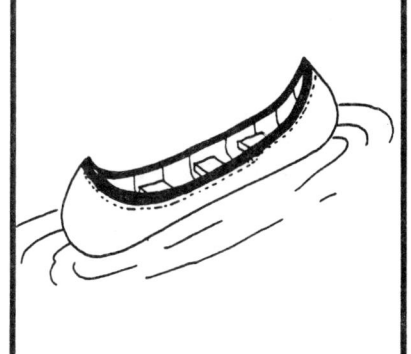   

Great Ideas for Teaching, Inc. 89 Developing Awareness of Similarities and Differences

Instructor's Worksheet

1. Flowers grow in a garden. Circle something that does not grow in a garden.

2. A person can wear a coat when it is cold outside. Circle something a person does not wear when it is cold outside.

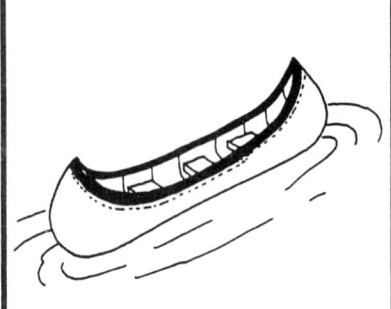

3. A canoe can float on the water. Circle something that cannot float on the water.

4. A bucket can be used to hold water. Circle something that cannot be used to hold water.

Great Ideas for Teaching, Inc.

Developing Awareness of Similarities and Differences

Name: _____ Date: _____

Great Ideas for Teaching, Inc.   91   Developing Awareness of Similarities and Differences

Instructor's Worksheet

1. A monkey has a tail. Circle something that does not have a tail.

2. Cereal is good to eat for breakfast. Circle something that is not good to eat for breakfast.

3. A bicycle has wheels. Circle something that does not have wheels.

4. Bricks can be used to build things. Circle something that can not be used to build things.

Great Ideas for Teaching, Inc.

Developing Awareness of Similarities and Differences

Name: _____ Date: _____

 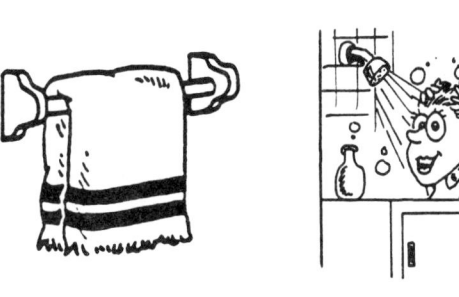 

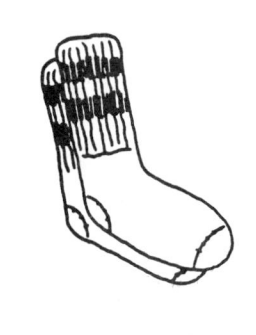   

Great Ideas for Teaching, Inc.

Developing Awareness of Similarities and Differences

Instructor's Worksheet

1. A bathtub can be found in a bathroom. Circle something that is not found in a bathroom.

2. A clown can be found at a circus. Circle something that is not found at a circus.

   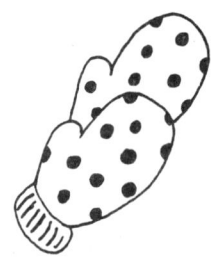

3. People wear socks on their feet. Circle something that is not worn on feet.

4. A baby can play with blocks. Circle something that a baby cannot play with.

Great Ideas for Teaching, Inc.   Developing Awareness of Similarities and Differences

Name: _____ Date: _____

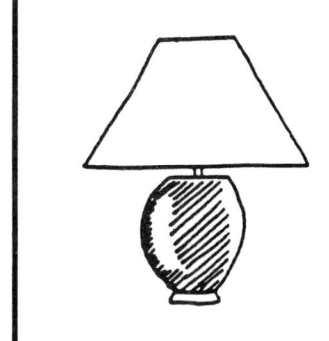 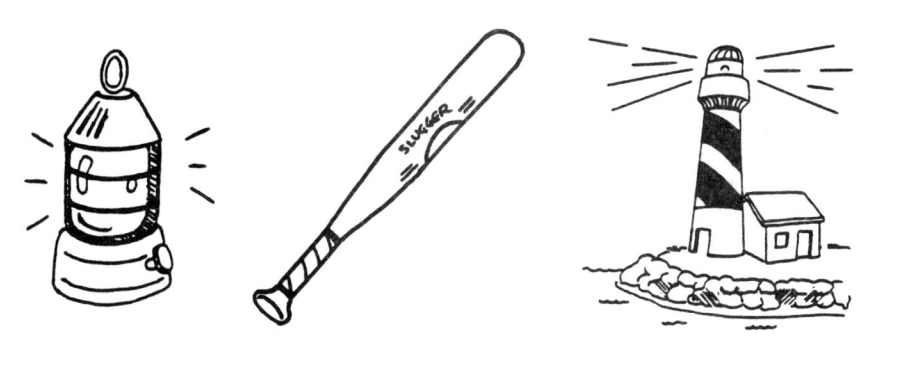

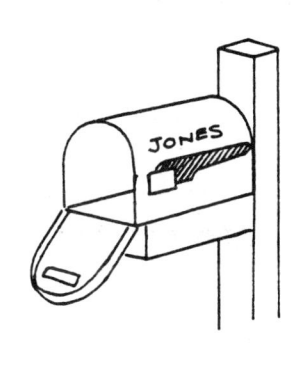 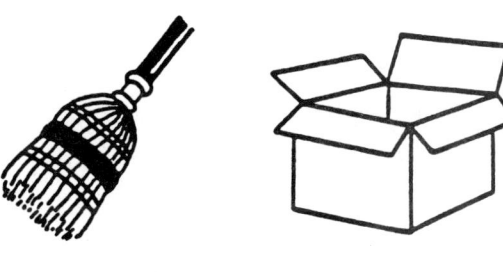 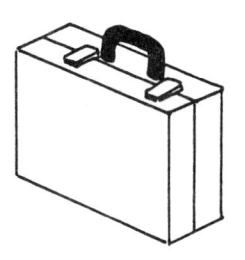

Great Ideas for Teaching, Inc. 95 Developing Awareness of Similarities and Differences

Instructor's Worksheet

1. A duck has feathers. Circle something that does not have feathers.

2. A lamp gives off light. Circle something that does not give off light.

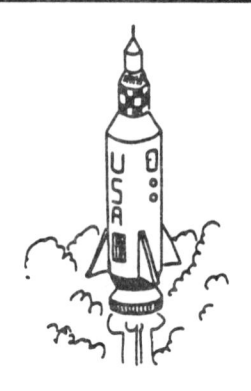   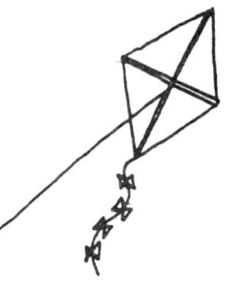

3. A rocket can fly fast through the air. Circle something that cannot fly fast through the air.

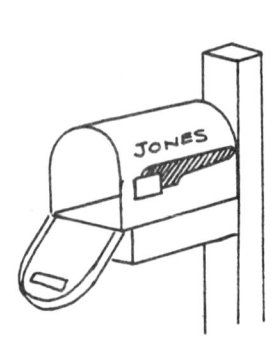   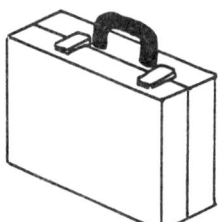

4. A mailbox opens and closes. Circle something that does not open and close.

Great Ideas for Teaching, Inc.

Developing Awareness of Similarities and Differences

Name: _____ Date: _____

 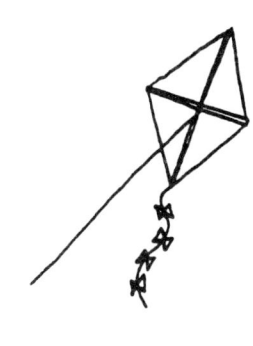 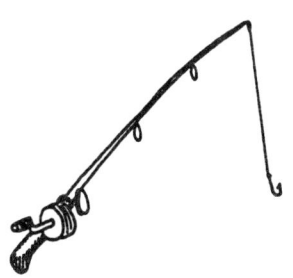 

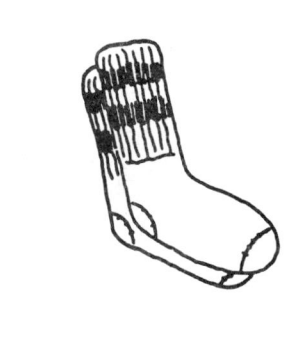   

Great Ideas for Teaching, Inc.

Developing Awareness of Similarities and Differences

Instructor's Worksheet

1. Dishes can be washed in a sink.. Circle something that cannot be washed in a sink.

2. A cow likes to eat grass. Circle something that does not like to eat grass.

 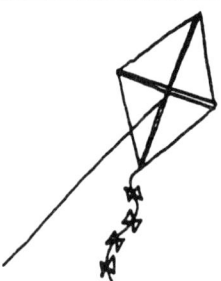 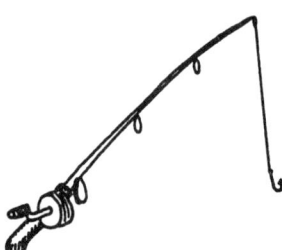 

3. A yo-yo has a long string. Circle something that does not have a long string.

4. Socks can be washed in a washing machine. Circle something that cannot be washed in a washing machine.

Name: _____ Date: _____

Great Ideas for Teaching, Inc.   99   Developing Awareness of Similarities and Differences

Instructor's Worksheet

1. A tractor moves slowly. Circle something that does not move slowly.

2. A tiger is dangerous. Circle something that is not dangerous.

3. A squirrel can climb a tree. Circle something that cannot climb a tree.

4. Milk can be stored in a refrigerator. Circle something that cannot be stored in a refrigerator.

Great Ideas for Teaching, Inc.   Developing Awareness of Similarities and Differences

Name: _____ Date: _____

 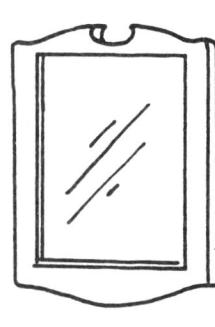 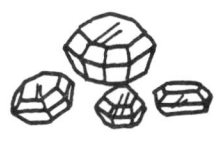 

Great Ideas for Teaching, Inc.   Developing Awareness of Similarities and Differences

Instructor's Worksheet

1. An elephant is big. Circle something that is not big.

2. Apples grow on trees. Circle something that does not grow on trees.

3. A boy has two legs. Circle something that has more than two legs.

 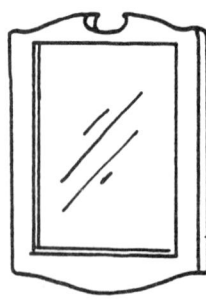 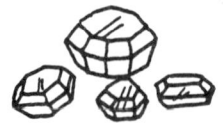 

4. A coin can be shiny. Circle something that is not shiny.

Great Ideas for Teaching, Inc.   102   Developing Awareness of Similarities and Differences

Name: _____ Date: _____

  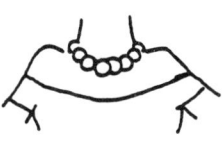 

 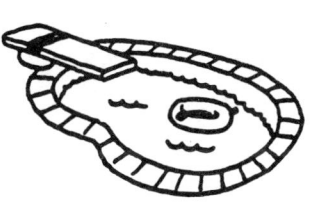 

Great Ideas for Teaching, Inc.   103   Developing Awareness of Similarities and Differences

Instructor's Worksheet

1. A bee can sting. Circle something that cannot sting.

2. You can buy a loaf of bread at a grocery store. Circle something you cannot buy at a grocery store.

  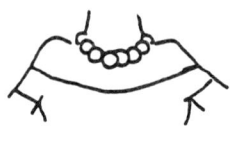 

3. A tie is worn around a neck. Circle something that cannot be worn around a neck.

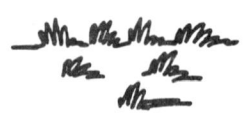  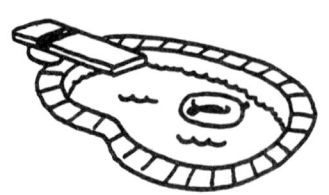 

4. Grass is found outside a house. Circle something that is not found outside a house.

Great Ideas for Teaching, Inc.

Developing Awareness of Similarities and Differences

Name: _____ Date: _____

Great Ideas for Teaching, Inc.

Developing Awareness of Similarities and Differences

Instructor's Worksheet

 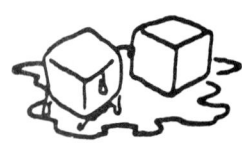 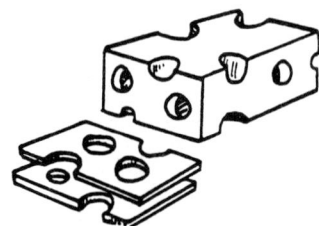 

1. Peanut butter is good to eat on a slice of bread. Circle something that is not good to eat on a slice of bread.

2. A bicycle has handlebars. Circle something that does not have handlebars.

  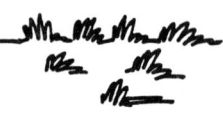 

3. Trees can grow in a forest. Circle something that cannot grow in a forest.

4. A bird has feathers. Circle something that does not have feathers.

Great Ideas for Teaching, Inc.   106   Developing Awareness of Similarities and Differences

Name: _____ Date: _____

Great Ideas for Teaching, Inc.   107   Developing Awareness of Similarities and Differences

Instructor's Worksheet

  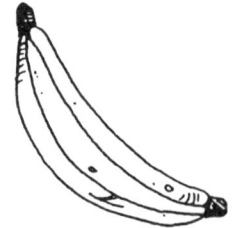 

1. Eggs are good to eat for breakfast. Circle something that is not good to eat for breakfast.

2. A hammer is used to build things. Circle something that is not used to build things.

3. Sand is found at the beach. Circle something that is not found at the beach.

4. Water is wet. Circle something that is not wet.

Great Ideas for Teaching, Inc.   Developing Awareness of Similarities and Differences

Name: _____ Date: _____

Great Ideas for Teaching, Inc. 109 <u>Developing Awareness of Similarities and Differences</u>

Instructor's Worksheet

 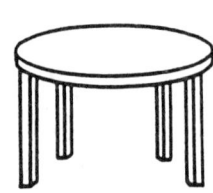  

1. A pillow is soft. Circle something that is not soft.

2. Ketchup is good to eat on a hamburger. Circle something that is not good to eat on a hamburger.

3. A car has tires. Circle something that does not have tires.

4. A pen can be used to write with. Circle something that cannot be used to write with.

Name: _____ Date: _____

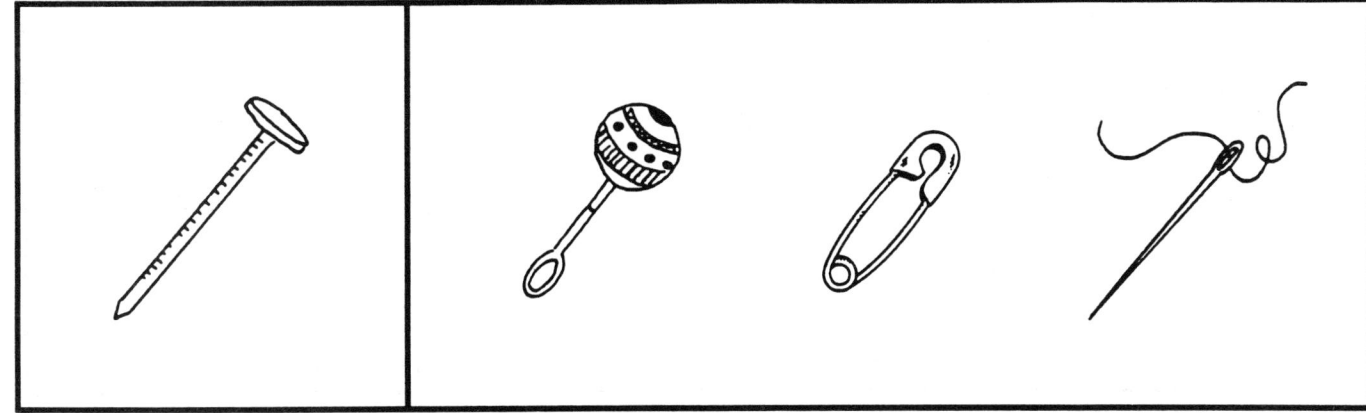

 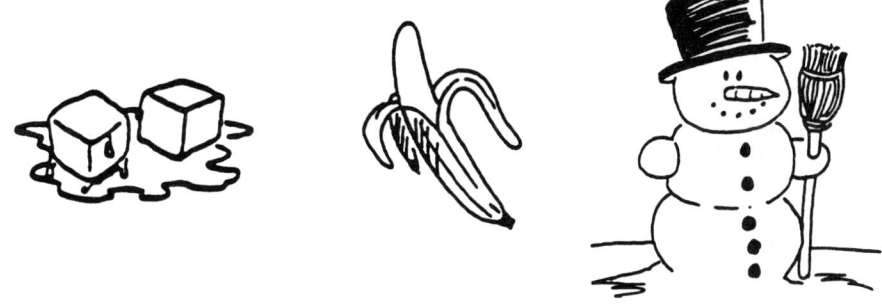

Great Ideas for Teaching, Inc.   111   Developing Awareness of Similarities and Differences

Instructor's Worksheet

   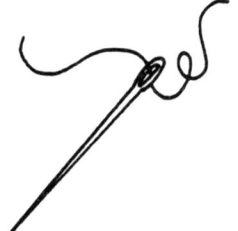

1. A nail is sharp. Circle something that is not sharp.

  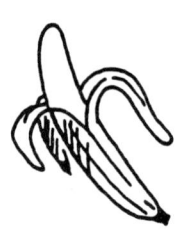 

2. Ice cream is frozen. Circle something that is not frozen.

3. A lion can live in a zoo. Circle something that does not live in a zoo.

4. A blackboard can be found in a classroom. Circle something that is not found in a classroom.

Great Ideas for Teaching, Inc.

Developing Awareness of Similarities and Differences

Name: _____ Date: _____

   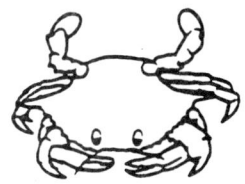

   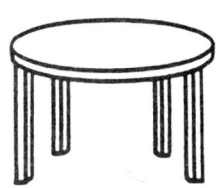

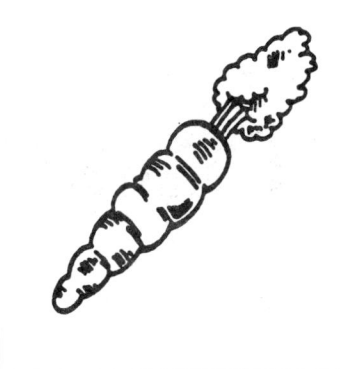   

Great Ideas for Teaching, Inc.

Developing Awareness of Similarities and Differences

Instructor's Worksheet

1. A fish lives in water. Circle something that does not live in water.

2. A stove is found in a kitchen. Circle something that is not found in a kitchen.

3. A raincoat can keep you dry. Circle something that cannot keep you dry.

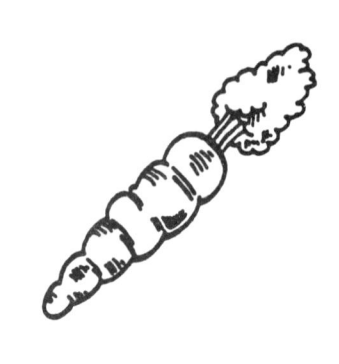   

4. A carrot is a vegetable. Circle something that is not a vegetable.

Name: _____ Date: _____

Great Ideas for Teaching, Inc.   115   Developing Awareness of Similarities and Differences

Instructor's Worksheet

1. A zebra has stripes. Circle something that does not have stripes.

2. An umbrella has a handle. Circle something that does not have a handle.

3. A policeman wears a uniform. Circle someone who does not wear a uniform.

4. Corn is yellow. Circle something that is not yellow.

Name: _____ Date: _____

 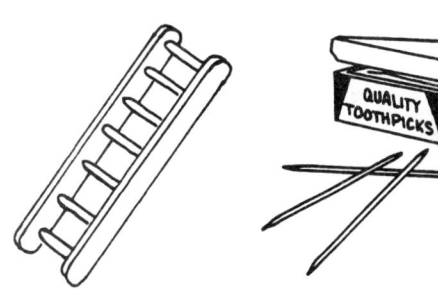 

Great Ideas for Teaching, Inc.　　　117　　Developing Awareness of Similarities and Differences

Instructor's Worksheet

1. A mouse has a long tail. Circle something that does not have a long tail.

2. A frog can hop. Circle something that cannot hop.

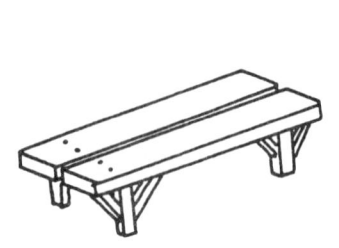 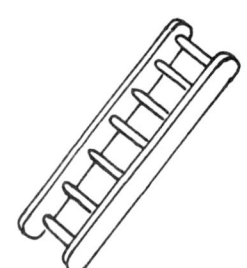  

3. A bench can be made of wood. Circle something that is not made of wood.

4. A leaf is very light. Circle something that is not very light.

Great Ideas for Teaching, Inc.   Developing Awareness of Similarities and Differences

Name: _____   Date: _____

Great Ideas for Teaching, Inc. 119 Developing Awareness of Similarities and Differences

Instructor's Worksheet

1. Milk is good to drink. Circle something that is not good to drink.

2. A stove is hot. Circle something that is not hot.

3. A seesaw goes up and down. Circle something that does not go up and down.

4. A rabbit has whiskers. Circle something that does not have whiskers.

Great Ideas for Teaching, Inc.

Developing Awareness of Similarities and Differences